ALL-AMERICAN GIRL

ALL-AMERICAN GIRL

Robin Becker

University of Pittsburgh Press

The publication of this book is supported by grants from the National Endowment for the Arts in Washington, D.C., a Federal agency, and the Pennsylvania Council on the Arts.

Published by the University of Pittsburgh Press, Pittsburgh, Pa. 15260
Copyright © 1996, Robin Becker
All rights reserved
Manufactured in the United States of America
Printed on acid-free paper
10 9 8 7 6 5 4 3 2

Library of Congress Cataloging-in-Publication Data and acknowledgments of permissions will be found at the end of this book.

A CIP catalogue record for this book is available from the British Library.

Eurospan, London

Book design: Frank Lehner

for Sally Greenberg and Carolyn Sachs

CONTENTS

ALL-AMERICAN GIRL

SHOPPING

If things don't work out
I'll buy the belt
with the fashionable silver buckle
we saw on Canyon Road.
If we can't make peace
I'll order the leather duster and swagger
across the plaza in Santa Fe,
cross-dressing for the girls.
If you leave I'll go back
for the Navaho blanket
and the pawn ring, bargain
with the old woman who will know
I intend to buy.
If you pack your things,
if you undress in the bathroom,
if you see me for what I am,
I'll invest in the folk art mirror
with the leaping rabbits
on either side, I'll spring
for the Anasazi pot with the hole
in the bottom where the spirit
of the potter is said to escape
after her death.

If you say you never intended
to share your life, I'll haunt the museum
shops and flea markets,
I'll don the Spanish riding hat,
the buckskin gloves with fringe at the wrists,
I'll step into the cowboy boots
tanned crimson and designed to make
any woman feel like she owns the street.
If you never touch me again,

I'll do what my mother did
after she buried my sister:
outfitted herself in an elegant suit
for the rest of her life.

THE CRYPTO-JEWS

This summer, reading the history of the Jews of Spain,
I learned Fra Alfonso listed "holding philosophical discussions"
as a Jewish crime. I think of the loud fights
between me and my father when he would scream that only a Jew
could love another Jew. I love the sad proud history
of expulsion and wandering, the Moorish synagogue walled
in the Venetian ghetto, persistence of study and text.
If we are the old Christ-killers on the handles of walking sticks,
we've walked the earth as calves, owls, and scorpions.
In New Mexico, the descendants of Spanish *conversos* come forth
to confess: tombstones in the yard carved with Stars of David,
no milk with meat, generations raised without pork.
What could it mean, this Hebrew script,
in grandmother's Catholic hand? Oh, New World, we drift
from eviction to eviction, go underground,
emerge in a bark on a canal, minister to kings, adapt to extreme
weather, peddle our goods and die into the future.

My Grandmother's Crystal Ball

Each summer we left Philadelphia
where our sweltering fathers swore they could drive their Falcons
around the rim of William Penn's fedora—a cast iron
version of their own—gigantic and
burning like a foundry in July.

Silver swells rolled forward like machinery
all day on the beach where we ran, five girl cousins too old
to be naked to the waist and wild as boys.
Late afternoon, the shadows of the great hotels
painted the sand.

After dark, our grandmother told us,
the water reached out predatory fingers and pulled
children under. Holding her hand, I heard hot, Dionysian laughter
rise from a blanket and saw the sandy, suntanned legs
of girls who sprinted up the stairs,

outlined by neon ads for peanuts and piers
that would, in a few years, disappear from Atlantic City.
I watched the sultry girls dash across the boardwalk
and drop to the street. My cousins yawned
and my grandmother's eyes met mine—

as if she knew that I was already running
with the wrong crowd,
as if she could see me leaning
against a polished bannister, staring
at a woman and letting her stare at me.

The Mystery, Then the Facts

As if my affection
    were holding you
        back as you strained

to go free
    like the filly who pulled
        me across the path

my dragging
    boots cut
        two trenches

As though you needed to say
    the harsh words
        of separation

like the rabbi
    making a distinction
        between the living and the dead

At dawn my friend and I
    skirt the marsh
        in our rain boots

and field jackets
    With binoculars I can't tell
        the difference:

what I see and what
    I want to see
        separation

or a prelude to commitment
    From the fog emerge
        individual trees

each comes toward me
        the mystery of your absence
            then the fact

    a life that took
        shape from a dream
            we spoke

into existence
        but could fashion
            only in words

Santo Domingo Feast Day

Think of the fox skins belted to the backs of the dancers

at Santo Domingo Pueblo, a thousand fox skins leaping.

The first year I heard the bells around their waists.

The second year I heard the drum inside my belly.

The third year we crossed our legs in the dirt, closed our eyes,

and sat through the dust storm. That year it turned holy.

That year the parrot feathers blew back to South America

and the dancers remained upright in wind that bent pine trees.

The gourd rattles turned to fruit. Aspen boughs became rifles.

We opened our eyes days later and they were still dancing,

we were still learning to empty our minds and listen.

I've been sitting in that dust for a decade, listening.

People I love have been shouting into the wind, saying

there are no remedies for the great sorrows,

only dancing and chanting, listening and waiting.

THE ELIMINATION OF FIRST THOUGHTS

I can imagine a composure that has nothing
to do with desire, though I think certain people
are born with it, like perfect pitch or
the ability to add large numbers in your head.
When his parents argued, a student once told me,
he and his brother would give each other addition
problems, impossibly long lists, and keep score
against the clock until the yelling stopped.
I wonder what he does now.
Or maybe it's not a gift but a practice,
like meditation or the martial arts: equanimity
of correct gesture and punch, the scream
that comes from the gut and wards off potential
attackers. I remember the tranquility of our teacher,
the female monk who shaved her head
and left Cambridge for the monastery in Kerala.
I thought she was crazy, renouncing the West
for the texts of Buddhist contemplation and study,
determined to erase longing and the body's hungers.
Remember how we snickered after class?
What did we know, doing T.M. for the first time,
trying it to save the relationship, already
looking around for the next thing and the next?

A History of Sexual Preference

We are walking our very public attraction
through eighteenth-century Philadelphia.
I am simultaneously butch girlfriend
and suburban child on a school trip,
Independence Hall, 1775, home
to the Second Continental Congress.
Although she is wearing her leather jacket,
although we have made love for the first time
in a hotel room on Rittenhouse Square,
I am preparing my teenage escape from Philadelphia,
from Elfreth's Alley, the oldest continuously occupied
residential street in the nation,
from Carpenters' Hall, from Congress Hall,
from Graff House where the young Thomas
Jefferson lived, summer of 1776. In my starched shirt
and waistcoat, in my leggings and buckled shoes,
in postmodern drag, as a young eighteenth-century statesman,
I am seventeen and tired of fighting for freedom
and the rights of men. I am already dreaming of Boston—
city of women, demonstrations, and revolution
on a grand and personal scale.
                        Then the maître d'
is pulling out our chairs for brunch, we have the
surprised look of people who have been kissing
and now find themselves dressed and dining
in a Locust Street townhouse turned café,
who do not know one another very well, who continue
with optimism to pursue relationship. *Eternity*
may simply be our mortal default mechanism
set on *hope* despite all evidence. In this mood,
I roll up my shirtsleeves and she touches my elbow.
I refuse the seedy view from the hotel window.

I picture instead their silver inkstands,
the hoopskirt factory on Arch Street,
the Wireworks, their eighteenth-century herb gardens,
their nineteenth-century row houses restored
with period door knockers.
Step outside.
We have been deeded the largest landscaped space
within a city anywhere in the world. In Fairmount Park,
on horseback, among the ancient ginkgoes, oaks, persimmons,
and magnolias, we are seventeen and imperishable, cutting classes
May of our senior year. And I am happy as the young
Tom Jefferson, unbuttoning my collar, imagining his power,
considering my healthy body, how I might use it in the service
of the country of my pleasure.

THE STAR SHOW

Though we're flat on our backs
at midnight
under the enormous sky, I know I'm really
in the Fels Planetarium
in Philadelphia, where I've come with the other
third-graders for the Star Show.
Tonight the trailing
blazes of white explode
across the darkness like firecrackers
and my companions *ooooh* and point
and say *over there,* though the words are too late
to be of use and hang
in the air much longer than light.

What I remember about the Star Show
is the commentator's calm voice,
the miracle spreading overhead
as he wooed us in plain English,
as if he didn't need special gear
to show us the sky's mysteries.
He needed only the reclining seats, the artificial
ceiling shuddering close with its countless stars,
our willingness to leave the known
earth, our parents, teachers, friends, ourselves
for this uncertain meeting in the dark.

He urged us to let our eyes adjust
for the journey, he asked us to relax
as the room began to spin and he whispered
in his knowledgeable voice about Jupiter.
Like my rabbi appearing suddenly in the dome
to discuss Moses, he explained with sorrow

that brilliant Galileo
had to retract his scientific
conclusions before the Inquisition.
This made us sad, for we already knew
that Galileo was right,
that four stars revolved around Jupiter
as the earth revolved around the sun.

And then, as though someone were shaking out a bedspread,
someone shook the sky and all the stars
shifted, it was winter, night of the lean wolf.
His voice grew cold and we buttoned our sweaters
because the temperature was falling, and we wanted
to follow him wherever he was going,
which was December.
                                    Across the mountain passes
we hunted bear; with the Hopis, we cured buffalo
hides and predicted the hour of sunrise.
Who didn't want to linger on that winter
mesa with the spotted ponies, so close to the stars?

There wasn't time. He was galloping toward
summer while I sat weeping for what I'd lost:
a glimpse of the sadness to come, the astronomer's
sure purpose. He guided the constellations
from early spring to June and then the sun
rose higher than we thought possible
and the longest day endured; he brought us into
a meadow drenched with light, but it was night,
we knew it, for now we could name every star.
How could he leave us here, now that we had become
his, now that he had asked us
to learn his heaven? As the chairs began to tilt

he threw the stars across the sky, flung meteors
carelessly and laughed a grown-up laugh.
He punctured the darkness with white bullets
and the kids began to shout.
The seats fell forward and the sun rose
in the auditorium, warming the air.
I sat bereft before the retreating stars.
Row by row we stood and blinked
into that autumn afternoon, as the ordinary jeers
and curses filled our mouths.

Solar

The desert is butch, she dismisses your illusions
about what you might do to make your life
work better, she stares you down and doesn't say
a word about your past. She brings you a thousand days,
a thousand suns effortlessly each morning rising.
She lets you think what you want all afternoon.
Rain walks across her mesa, red-tailed hawks
writhe in fields of air, she lets you look at her.
She laughs at your study habits, your orderly house,
your need to name her "vainest woman you've ever met."
Then she turns you toward the voluptuous valleys,
she gives you dreams of green forests,
she doesn't care who else you love.
She sings in the grass, the sagebrush, the small trees
struggling and the tiny lizards scrambling
up the walls. You find her when you're ready
in the barbed wire and fence posts, on the scrub where you walk
with your parched story, where she walks, spendthrift,
tossing up sunflowers, throwing her indifferent
shadow across the mountain. Haven't you guessed?
She's the loneliest woman alive but that's her gift;
she makes you love your own loneliness,
the gates to darkness and memory. She is your best, indifferent
teacher, she knows you don't mean what you say.
She flings aside your technical equipment,
she requires you to survive in her high country
like the patient sheep and cattle who graze and take her
into their bodies. She says *lightning,* and
get used to it. Her storms are great moments
in the history of American weather, her rain remakes the world,
while your emotional life is run-off from a tin roof.

Like the painted clown at Picuris Pueblo
who started up the pole and then dropped into the crowd,
anonymous, she paws the ground, she gallops past.
What can you trust? This opening, this returning,
this arroyo, this struck gong inside your chest?
She wants you to stay open like the hibiscus
that opens its orange petals for a single day.
At night, a fool, you stand on the chilly mesa,
split open like the great cleft of the Rio Grande Gorge,
trying to catch a glimpse of her, your new, long-term companion.
She gives you a sliver of moon, howl of a distant dog,
windy premonition of winter.

BRISK AUTUMN AND THE QUERULOUS TREES

crack. Who tucked the wind below
the horse's tail? She sidesteps,
ears flat, and bucks once,
twice, for the feel of her back
slapping air.
One by one the smooth green hills
ripen and flare, this is the gathering place
where summer holds and gives, where
every field of goldenrod
is a metaphor for loss.
You show me the path you reclaimed from brush,
the bushes finished now, harvesting
a few red berries before the frost.
I want to say something about being
a woman, middle-aged.
Instead we walk the ridge
with your tireless dog and praise
the snug farmhouses, the orderly
outbuildings and neat squares
of russet and sage already turning
brittle, the color of winter.

We Thought of Each Other as Food

—*after David Shapiro*

We thought of each other as food, taut skin
of the apple burnished with stars We thought of each other
as France, Brittany blue and Provençal roads, postcards
from the vast Midi of your mouth We thought of each other
as fact, a fanlight above the boathouse door
and then the door opened and we sailed
in the parallel hulls of feminine
endings, catamaran, raft of logs lashed together
We thought of each other as fish in fathoms of light
where we glistened and swam, in the dangerous rooms
and coral reefs where sea horses glittered
If I thought at all, my God, how could I
think when your hips churned, while the presses ran,
while someone on the night shift took a break
and stared at the summer constellations,
hovering like a map of the rest of her life?
We thought of each other as fiction
and wrote our story with kisses,
our characters spoke and revised their opinions,
each night they broke free from convention
We thought of each other as Ferris wheel and fairground
on the turning axes of our bodies

PORT-AU-PRINCE, 1960

My sister and I stand at the ship's rail
and watch the Greek sailors
hurl buckets of water on the gangplank.
The drops glow and fall in the bright sun,
here where they manufacture light
and salt air for our happiness.
Next, they unfurl a heavy red carpet which we know
is for us, for our shoes, since our pleasure
and comfort are very dear to them.
All morning, black boys have been diving for change
from splintering rowboats.
I try to imagine how their heads feel
miles underwater where they must swim
to find the dimes. Against the azure Caribbean Sea
their bodies shine . . . they shoot up
like geysers, like fountains of oil, holding one
fist above their heads to signify success. Again
and again they go down to the bottom
to collect the silver coins,
and I notice that they have surrounded us
in their rowboats and canoes, and now they are clapping
and yelling, urging all the white people crowded
at the rail to throw, to throw, to empty our pockets.
Blue-black, they drift in circles, one at the oars, the other
poised to dive, and in my child's mind their screams and whistles
are cries of anger. The great ship inches steadily
toward shore, toward the dense jungle, the golf courses
and tennis courts, restaurants and clubs.
The black boys retreat in their tiny boats,
as our pastel crowd pushes forward. I squeeze
my sister's hand; we have been told to stay

together, to walk directly behind our parents,
to avoid eye contact. Before I step onto the island,
I know that I am different from the people
who live here, I know that I have something another child needs.

QUAKER MEETING, THE SIXTIES

Seeing my friend's son in his broad-brimmed hat
and suspenders, I think of the Quakers
who lectured us on nonviolent social action
every week when I was a child. In the classrooms
we listened to those who would not take up arms,
who objected, who had accepted alternative
service in distant work camps and showed
slides of hospitals they helped to build.
On Wednesdays, in Meeting for Worship,
when someone rose to speak,
all the energy in the room
flew inside her mouth, empowering her to tell
what she had seen on her brief
encounter with the divine: sometimes, a parable,
a riddle, a kindness. The fall that we were seventeen,
we scuffed our loafers on the gravelly path
from the Meetinghouse, while maple and elm
leaves sailed around our shoulders
like tiny envelopes, our futures sealed inside.
Despite the war in Vietnam, I felt safer
than I ever would again. Perhaps
those aged, protective trees had cast a spell
on us, or maybe the nonviolent Quaker God
had set up a kingdom right there—
suburban Philadelphia. Looking back, I see how
good deeds and thoughts climbed with us to the attic
room for Latin, descended to the gym for sports,
where we hung from the praiseworthy scaffolds
of righteous behavior. We prepared to leave
for college, armed with the language of the American
Friends and the memories of Thanksgiving
dinners we'd cooked for the unfortunates:
borrowing our parents' cars to drive

downtown to the drop-off point, racing back
to play our last field hockey match. Grim center forwards
shook hands before the whistle, the half-backs'
knee-pads strapped on tight; one varsity team vanquished another.

Villanelle for a Lesbian Mom

It wasn't love but chance and rather sweet—
your newly weaned son asleep in his crib, your breasts too tender
to be touched. And touch itself, too early, indiscreet.

Who would have believed that over a drink and something to eat
you'd lose your car, locked in overnight? Parking offender,
it wasn't love but chance and rather sweet.

So you found yourself in bed with a grown-up, a feat
of sorts. My recent loss had left me wondering when I'd mend or
want to be touched. I wanted you, however indiscreet.

Your small son breathed and coughed. I tried to sleep
but couldn't ignore what your body engendered
in mine. It wasn't love but chance and strangely sweet.

I like your name; you're used to mine, ironic repeat
of your old lover's. With so few facts ought two people surrender
to touch? (Better to date, slow down, try to be discreet.)

OK, let's walk around the pond, take a few months or weeks
to study each other and see what portends or
not. It wasn't love but chance and rather sweet.
I'm *moved* by you as well as touched: shy *and* indiscreet.

IN PIETRASANTA

—*for Marianne Weil*

After the war, the buoyant Italians
came down from the hills, they resumed their noisy
motorbikes and hard laughter at Bar Nella.
Stonecarvers returned to the dust-filled
studios in their little newspaper hats,
and I recall their small coughs,
white lungs, white aprons, and rickety bicycles
leaning against an ancient wall, mottled
with an ochre patina, a mustard patina . . .
In your old Fiat, we swept around the dark
curves of cracked stone plastered
with black and white death notices, like circus posters
advertising an upcoming show.
Shadows of umbrella pines fell
across the beach in Viareggio, silhouettes clustered
and waved in the wind as we sped by.
Sometimes, next to the fragrant rosemary, we'd stumble
on a box of tomatoes—hard, dark planets—
left by your neighbor, the quiet farm woman.
The walled town on top of the hill
sparkled with tiny lights, while next door,
at the bar, the shouts of foundry workers filled
our dreams with violence. Each morning you left
in your white T-shirt to wrestle and polish the bronze,
returning for the lunch I'd fix, the wife,
who sets the steaming pasta on the table.
Two women, we tried to shape our days to the rhythms
of that town: noon whistle, long afternoons shuttered
against the heat, evening promenades down Via di Mezzo.
That was the summer I couldn't work and fled

in the rain to Florence where I wandered around
the piazzas and museums, wondering what
to do next. We took your mother to Venice—
though we were hardly speaking—because
you thought she was going to die
without seeing how a whole city could reflect
upon itself. For months, I'd wanted one thing: I wanted you
to go painting with me, in a field, or an olive grove.
I wanted us to be together with our paper and brushes,
creating something at the same time.
The night before I left for the States, you said
OK, come on, and in the dark you led me
to the field behind the Romanesque church. There,
we spread out our colors, all black, and began.

HAIRCUT ON VIA DI MEZZO

The brisk beautician nodded toward a chair
and twirled a pair of scissors, one hand in the damp hair
of the woman who ran the milk store down the street
I'd frequented all summer. I took a seat. To wait.
                              In town a week,
I'd gone for mozzarella, bewildered by the array,
and eager to please you with my choice. I studied the coy
Italian yogurts, their bright letters, milk cartons,
glass jugs of cream. When my turn came, I tried to explain
that I didn't know what kind—*bufalo, misto*—to buy.
She narrowed her eyes. *With whom do you stay?* she asked in Italian.
Surprised, I said your name, trying to frame our friendship and
disguise what I knew you wanted to hide. *Misto,* she said
clearly and repeated your name. *She prefers misto.*
Every few days, when we ran out of eggs or milk, I returned;
she called me *Americana* and asked after you, *bella Marianna.*

Listen, everybody knew everything. At the *lavanderia,*
in the steam, the singing Englishman who washed our sheets
and jeans showed his esteem by chatting with me
about your old girlfriend, said she used to complain
about her shirts. (God knows I'd mend mine myself
before I'd say a word.) In line at the Post Office,
I asked for my mail and got yours. For free, the grocer
bagged an aging bunch of leeks, told me to tell you:
make soup. Nights, we sat on the stoop of our seventeenth-
century home, planned a trip to Rome, struggled to get along.
Only the merchants found our work-vacation amusing.
Between us, conversation had become
a series of sparring gestures.

The eight-year-old rose for her haircut
and siblings turned to stare. On one side of me sat
her brothers; on the other, her parents, and an aged grandmother

dressed for the affair in black. The cutter beckoned
with a long finger, and I saw, suddenly, a rope uncoil
and hair twist down the child's back to the floor.
When the scissors snapped and the first hank of hair fell
to the marble tiles, the girl whirled, the whites
in her eyes flashing. I saw tears bubble
and slide down her face as she fixed her gaze on her father.
Cool and serene, he nodded to her, his youngest child,
and she, obedient, knowing what had to be, leaned
toward the blades and turned her wildness inside.

FAMILY ROMANCE

1

We were still trying to talk about having children—
still believed that talk could hatch an answer each
of us could claim—the night of the outdoor concert

by the female rockabilly group with an unfamiliar name.
Hoisting knapsacks and picnic baskets, we joined the gathering
crowd, couples hurrying to stake out a good square of lawn.

We got enough space to eat and stretch. Then, we took turns
leaving. I made some excuse about going for drinks and stepped
carefully over wine bottles and sweaters, thinking

about the way certain horses under saddle
will gradually work the bit and extend their necks
so that the riders, unconscious, allow the leather

reins to slide through their fingers, until the horses gain
their heads, and bolt—riders thrown, bridle flapping.
Trainers say these horses learn to swindle

their freedom and can be taught to take the bit, to round
their necks, to sense the opening—like fine athletes
everywhere looking for the main chance   and let it pass.

2

Next to us a family from France unpacked their supper
and shared with us their Camembert. They'd forgotten
warm clothes; I offered them our surplus.

First, one accepted a pair of socks; another took a sweatshirt;
Soon, they looked like us in our bright American gear—
parkas and buntings curled against each other.

Like curious relatives from out of town, they were
enthusiastic, generous, but unprepared for the weather, and I felt
protective, wanted them to have the feather vests, to stay warm.

The sky filled with stars, the musicians played, I watched
the French smoke and smile, whispering to one another, passing
a bottle of wine along the row and behind, to us.

Later, when the concert ended, they thanked us and returned
our clothes, and I had a moment of sadness
amid all the thanking, as if now there would be no one

who needed anything from us. Free, I thought of that horse,
too unpredictable for a child, a mount who could fool
the most observant rider. You led the way to the parking lot

in silence, wondering how you would ever have a family of your own.
On the way we passed the French—now all bare legs and arms—
huddled together, a knot of foreign joy in the cold American air.

Peter Pan in North America

Mary Martin, leader of the Lost Boys,
when you flew across the stage in drag,
in your tattered forest suit, teasing Hook,
some of us recognized you. Girl-boy, darling,
you refused to grow into any version
of manhood, while we cheered at the play

in New York, 1960, tomboys pulled from play
to put on dresses and sit among the feckless boys.
Years later, we cultivated our baby butch versions
of Peter before our mirrors. That day, we couldn't drag
ourselves from our seats. "You liked the play, darling?"
our knowing mothers asked. We dangled from the hook

of their question, the answer as overdetermined as Hook's
effeminate ways. Being a boy was best. Second best, we'd play
Peter in school plays, flirt with our Wendy Darlings,
and strap on toy sabers like pirates taking Lost Boys
hostage. After all, Mary Martin could fly, take a drag
from a pipe, dance with her shadow, reject predictable versions

of femaleness. Call it chutzpah or perversion,
we imagined ourselves. breasts bound, hooked
to guy wires, smartly dressed in roguish drag.
We took our own message from the play:
if grown-up, gendered roles awaited all girls and boys,
then woe to her whom he called "darling."

When the time came, we called each other "darling"
and fell into our own problematic diversions
and girl-girl relations. Next door the gay boys
camped it up, swishing around in capes like Hook.
Now we've got adult cult artists to play
the gender-bending game, we know the world needs drag

queens, he-shes, and transvestites at the drag
ball. Behind the hetero scrim, Mr. and Mrs. Darling,
fly erotic creatures of every sexual preference who play
havoc with your repressed aversions.
Skirt and slip, tank and tights, drop the baited hook
and we'll all bite—girls, boys,

everything in between. Drag revealed our own inversions
long before the Darlings were upstaged by Hook,
and grown-up play separated the Marys from the boys.

SPIRITUAL MORNING

I am as virtuous as a rabbinical student
after my morning run, God in the body awake, God
of the May apple and wild ginger. Even the little
stiff hands of the whistle pig reach
toward me in death's perfection. Once,
in Katmandu at dawn, I watched a monk in a saffron robe
brush his teeth on the roof of a temple and spit—
and from his mouth flew peach and azure birds
fluttering in the milky sweetness of the air.

        This morning of Pennsylvania
woodchuck and wild geranium, I grasp the
connection among all sentient beings and feel
communion with the wretched of all species and the dead.
The orange swallowtail looping overhead, for example,
is really my old grandmother, back to remind me
to learn Yiddish, the only international language.
I'd like her to sit on my finger
so we could talk face-to-face, but she flies
out of sight, shouting, *Big talker! Don't run on busy streets!*

OPALS

—for Tamar Craig

I knew the hard winter of sapphires
set within gold claws,
amber and pipestone strung on gut,
fringed pouches stuffed with hash.
Separate, separate, I urged her
that summer of Woodstock,
when I lied to get the car
and draped my love beads
around the neck of someone else's sister.

In a hayloft in Ohio
my friend lifted three bales
to show me a litter of week-old kittens,
each pair of eyes infected with a slimy mucus.
Their pupils swam in opaque opal membranes
and they would have gone blind
if she had not pulled an eyedropper
of antibiotics from her jacket,

doing what the mother cat
could not do, what the owners
would not trouble themselves to do,
doing what a sister or friend
might do if she took the time
to attend the wayward, opalescent
unhappiness in this world.

Too Jewish

You'll be more yourself, my Bubbie argued.
I already am myself, I shouted.
She turned away. *I'll pay!* she cried,
hurling her last old woman's weapon.
In the Depression, her three daughters marched
before the knife, the gleam of good marriages
in her prescient eye.
My sister only wanted a date.

Years later, in Jerusalem, I bought a Star
of David and hung it around my neck.
Why so big? she asked. *The whole world
has to know you're Jewish?*

When the bandages came off
my sister's nose still lacked perfection.
Look, he did the best he could,
Bubbie snorted, always a defender of doctors.
I was their child: half my life
I believed I could fix a problem
by cutting it away. In the name of love
we draw a blade across the beloved's face.

TELLING THEM APART

After she died I did not help my mother
and her sister sort through the closets
of Ralph Lauren dresses. I did not wrap
the Delft figurines and Wedgwood boxes
in *The Philadelphia Inquirer*.
The battered women's shelter came
with a truck for the bed and sofa.
The Salvation Army came for clothing and underwear.
The maid answered the door in one of her sweaters,
my mother wore her flowered jumpsuits,
gold chains, opal ring.
I took the Cross pen she bought for herself and worried

I would lose it. Then I lost it.
At the stationery store in Cambridge
I bought another, identical,
not caring that it wasn't the one
she'd carried in her leather purse.
Silver, like the first, it took the same
soft tip insert, had the same lettering
across the top, just like the one my sister
left to me, no one could tell them apart,
like us, at six and eight in the old pictures,
wearing identical dresses
with smocking across the chest.

Risk

The kildeer nested on the ground—
seconds from the horses' hooves
and the graceful arcs of the canter.
Each time we rounded the turn, she stood
over her speckled eggs (I could
see them from my horse's back)
and made a display
of her fierce white feathers.
How I admired her! Audacious
before the iron shoes!

CONTRADANCING IN NELSON, N.H.

—for Leslie Lawrence

It was a ragged crew, just like you'd said—
some hippies, gents and ladies, little kids.
On stage, our landlord fiddled in his red

T-shirt, a country maestro, as he slid
his fingers up and down the viol's neck.
The barefoot caller, a local who lived

for the do-si-dos, had a strange inflect-
ion, strange to me, that is. You pointed out
the folks you recognized, oddballs protect-

ed by rural tradition. With a shout
the allemandes began, and a stout man,
pony-tailed, masking a Talmudic pout,

bowed politely and requested your hand.
Couples lined up according to gender
and flew through steps at the caller's command.

The music roused me, summer pretender
to the country life, and I slapped my knee
like the townies who could still remember

Nelson's young years, when locals didn't flee
the Saabs and Volvos racing down the hills.
In cut-offs, a musician tuned his C.

The dancers drank from bottles perched on sills.
We swatted at mosquitos as we looked
at the crowd, noting the women in frills,

the men in funky summer get-up, hooked
on Birkenstocks and silk-screened cow T-shirts.
When the caller started again, you booked

me with the scholar who would have been hurt
if I'd refused. "But I'm a beginner,"
I demurred. He smiled benignly. No flirt,

he explained that in Nelson a sinner
(we dipped past and came back where we started)
is one who can't turn novice to winner.

Afterwards, I thanked him and we parted.
Back on my bench, I wondered: is *she* gay?
When I mentioned the idea you smarted.

"You can't tell by looking," I heard you say.
"These local women defy all the rules.
They're married, ride tractors, and put up hay."

A blond-haired guy asked you to dance, a school-
boy type, a graceful libertarian,
befitting New Hampshire tradition. Fool-

ishly, I didn't ask the fine woman
on my left, afraid to be the only
all-female couple on the floor. You'd been

asked to dance by several girls. A homely-
faced Ginger Rogers put us all to shame
with her sister. Had I only known we

were honored guests, that nothing could restrain
their generous impulse to include
us, I might have found the will to detain

that dark-haired beauty who, spinning 'round, wooed
by someone else, promenaded like a
queen on the arm of a girl, bright eyes glued

to each other. Then up to the mike a
new caller took his turn at the last dance—
traditional waltz; we rose (despite a

brief hesitation) and shot a last glance
at the couples who swept 'cross the floor,
waltzing to the "live free or die" romance.

THE WOMAN QUESTION

Lying awake, I'm still looking for signs
on the winter beach, where I found two sand dollars
of equal size and weight. Boarded-up, my heart,
like a summer house closed till spring.
Past pier and fishing tackle. Waves slapping.
Enough beach glass to build an opaque city.
People with large dogs running and small dogs wearing
red bandannas. Sea gulls that plunged to their deaths
or fell mercifully from the sky stricken with heart attacks.
The salt water was wrecking my boots, but I believed
I could clear my head if I just kept walking
and muttering my questions and objections: *Should I leave you?*
Should I stay? At the west end I hoped the shoreline
would finish sharply, but it lingered on, levitated
into sandbars and bleached landing docks.
Ropes coiled beneath the sand like serpents
and I almost broke my neck, I swear.
A man on the beach stood like a stake, skipping stones.
He wore the hard crease of his body like a fence.
I wanted a body incapable of reproducing
grief or inexorable questions of itself.
I wanted to surrender the female requirement to care
always more for someone else. I turned back no more
resolved than the long-distance cyclist whose sleep
returns her to the uphill climb,
repeating in dreams the all-day training rides.
In the distance, figures bent double over rakes,
combing the sand as a mother combs her child's hair.
When I was a child, I wanted to be the boy across the street
who hung upside down from a tree and didn't care
that his shirt fluttered over his bare chest.
I carried broken birds home in a box

and sat over that box with an eyedropper, waiting
for a cry. When one died, I tried to find another
to love and I learned to breathe quietly, to replicate
a nest, to anticipate need. I heard a woman's voice
in the tide, the *give, give, give* pushing up
the beach and taking every glittering thing back.
Light exposed the underside of pilings, upended rowboats
and cleaved a bright path that felt like the future.
In the sun's wake I almost succeeded in becoming
a boy, fastening myself to a tree limb, then to solitude,
then to loneliness, then to nothing at all.

WHEN SOMEONE DIES YOUNG

When someone dies young
a glass of water lives
in your grasp like a stream.
The stem of a flower
is a neck you could kiss.
When someone dies young
and you work steadily
at the kitchen table
in a house calmed by music
and animals' breath,
you falter at the future,
preferring the reliable past,
films you see over and over
to feel the inevitable
turning to parable, characters
marching with each viewing
to their doom.
When someone dies young
you want to make love furiously
and forgive yourself.
When someone dies young
the great religions welcome you,
a supplicant begging with your bowl.
When someone dies young
the mystery of your own
good luck finds a voice
in the bird at the feeder.
The strict moral lesson
of that life's suffering
takes your hand, like a ghost,
and vows companionship
when someone dies young.

BICYCLE DAYS

I heard the jerk
of a chain and turned;
in your palm, the derailleur
cracked in two. *Metal fatigue,*
you called to me, miles
from the car, halfway
into the day's ride.
By what magic did you conjure
a teenage boy, strolling down the hill, .
Marlboros snug in his T-shirt's folds?
I can fix it, he said. *Wait here.*
Call it karma or luck, he returned
with the part, knelt on the ground
and pulled from his pockets the tools.
Another save.
In an hour we were pumping up the hill.

We pedal into our old ways.
A bend in the road draws
us to a fishing village, a country store,
where I admire jars of local jam
and you order sandwiches.
Panniers, old cycling shorts, grease-
stained gloves: I follow
the bumblebee-yellow helmet
I bought you for a birthday before we left
each other. A year later, we're trading
stories—lovers we've taken, towns we explored
with other people, jobs we didn't get.
Bicycle days. Pedalling hard, uphill,
I know your new apartment fills
with things we never had room for. Forgive me.
A couch, beloved paintings, cupboards of dishes

recovered from friends' basements.
Oh, sweet one,
what fatigue finally forced us apart?
On the beach that day
only the hardy
Maine children made it
into the frigid water.
We watched a boy, legs twisted
from birth, stab the sand unsteadily.
His mother carried the walker
he discarded, and you spoke
of her patience, the way she did not rush
the boy but absorbed the gazes of the curious,
the way a lead apron will take the lethal rays.
I return to the memory
as I return to many others—guarded,
with my old fear that events
and the people inside them
will ask more of me
than I'm prepared to give.
You asked more of me: demanded
I ride the forty-five miles
and complete the day's loop, stay
with you and raise a child.

By morning, dark clouds drifted
over the route, but you insisted
we complete what we started.
Twenty miles into the ride, a steady rain
oiled the asphalt, dripped
from your glasses. *I'm hitching back,*
I said, half-serious, half-thinking
I'd convince you to quit.

We're riding, you said. *Trust me.* I followed,
angry, frightened of skidding, our positions
fixed as the map in your mind.
We cycled through soggy towns,
past white church steeples gone
gray in the Maine afternoon.
You'll be glad you did it, you shouted
as I walked my bike on a slippery turn.
Over dinner we toasted
the route, the rain, the ride.
Beloved, what fear held me back? What kept
me from trusting when you only wanted
to keep going, to bring us home,
to usher us into a life
we could hold, tangible as the handlebars
in our four hands?

THE RIBBON

We earned them
by completing the course
without error,
by showing the best form
at the walk, trot, and canter.
Blue, red, yellow, and white,
the ribbons fluttered
from the horses' bridles
as we trotted
proudly from the ring.

Each night before sleep
my mother removes
from her blouse
the piece of black fabric.
The dark threads
have started to fray.
In the morning
she will pin it to her dress
and everyone she meets will know
she has completed one life
and entered the ring
for another.

HOLD BACK

Like afternoon shadows on October adobes, she will fall
   and fall on me, wind fluttering white at the window,
      smell of piñon fires and first snow

on the mountain. Cool blue altitudes we drive,
   down here we burn, let silence rain its quiet
      weather, let her suntanned arm graze mine

with its peachbloom glaze; I know how to walk away
   and come back shining. In time she will open her shirt,
      she will show me her neck, she will close her eyes.

But we're not yet lovers, we're seekers from the valleys,
   laden with turquoise and silver, interested
      in each other the way traders fall in love

with a beautiful bracelet, the one they haven't had
   and still think will make a difference. But we're not
      thinking of the future—that's one of the conditions—

I'm tracing her palm with my finger and feeling
   the Rio Grande rush over the autumn stones. I'm kissing
      the inside of her elbow, the moccasin-soft skin

is a song I heard at the pueblo when the women
   danced together the small, mysterious movements.
      Soon she'll lie on her stomach with her chest pressed

into the thin sheet and I'll climb
   to her back, freckled with summer
      light. Impatient, she throws her head left and right,

she wants me to begin, she's been waiting
    all afternoon for my hand
        at the base of her spine,

so I hold back. All we know of pleasure
    is pleasure delayed, the fine
        restraint which once given over is gone.

MIDNIGHT SWIM

She likes the comely shape of the copper beech
and notes the wedge of sky that shows where the tree
received stigmata. I like to watch her
walk up the path because she is beautiful and
sees beauty where I see sadness: in the retreating summer
night, in the night of the pond's enormous, still eye,
in the amphitheater of bullfrog and treefrog and peeper,
in the silver steam coming off the water, in the arc
of the diving body disappearing, in the splash of a creature
nearing we name turtle or snake. The floating dock
drifts with its jealous reflection appearing like a face.
And I who have no claim on this woman or this lake
take the measure of the summer from the fireflies—
luminous against the dark trees—and the slowly revolving
dock I dream free from its moorings by morning.

Dreaming at the Rexall Drug

In Wyoming, at the confluence
of Clear and Piney creeks, I find myself
watching low clouds mass above the Bighorns.
If I were to get on the bicycle
and ride to Buffalo,

I'd saunter into the Rexall Drug
and order a root beer float, I'd fill out
a contest form to win a thoroughbred,
as I did every week in my eighth year,
in love with the bay in the plate glass window.

In Buffalo, Wyoming, an America
my Russian grandmother never imagined,
we are standing before the cosmetics
counter, and she is testing Revlon
lipsticks to find the perfect shade of peach.

I drift toward the comic books where Lois Lane
is repeatedly rescued and flies—
past skyscrapers and suspension bridges—
as I do in my dreams.
My grandmother takes my hand and we walk.

At the house it's 1955 and
my father has the thick black hair he lost
before I was born. He leads us to the
patio where Chinese lanterns sway
like soft paper crowns. All the neighbors

I will grow to love are laughing and floating
in the buoyant atmosphere, and here comes
my mother in a party dress, holding
my baby sister. I've not learned to read
their faces for bankruptcy or grief.

As far as I know, everyone will live
forever, and little girls like me
will continue to win racehorses
from Rexall, where my grandmother will stand,
twisting lipstick tubes, discovering one

imperfect color after another.

MEETING THE GAZE OF THE GREAT HORNED OWL

From a distant room
in the woods
the owl burst down,
flung herself like a skydiver and hovered
above me. I covered my face with my arms and ran
toward her—strange—because
I was afraid.

I had disturbed the quiet
of the feathered one
who rested now, overhead, in a dead tree
where jays and flickers pecked and cried.
The owl acknowledged each note, each tiny, colored movement,
by twisting, on a calm trivet, her troubled head,
the dappled body perfectly still,

and I admit that I wanted
the creature's attention, to compete
with the smaller birds,
so I made my human noises and the owl attended,
turned her brown, comprehending eyes
down to me and met my stare.
I moved my arms—slowly—in an awkward imitation

of flight,
pawing the air like an animal awakened abruptly
or just beginning
to know the power of her wings.
I held the owl's gaze as I swayed
and wondered what she saw:
something large straining to rise

and failing. I thought of my younger sister, dead,
and I wanted her back, to show her,
as I never did in life,
how fear and longing sometimes go together,
how one small percussive surprise
in the trees can turn you
from one self to another, this one with wings.

FROM TAOS TO SANTA FE

—for Nora Ryerson

The South Santa Fe Road
veers east, and then the Rio Grande Gorge State Park
offers desert on all sides.
I drive the strip
of highway, Tres Piedras, Abiquiu
in the southern distance.

Inevitable rain
runs off the miles of sage, chamisa, land
fenced with barbed wire, holding what?
No animals
may be pastured here—no water, no shade
in this punishing place.

The horseshoe curve spirals
through a mountain pass above the desert
and then descends to seven
thousand feet, where
famous piñon pines dot pink and gray slopes.
A logging truck slows me.

I tailgate through Pilar,
a tiny town whose river traffic keeps
two bed and breakfasts busy:
hungry and tired
the river rats haul rafts from the Rio Grande.
Water meanders close

on my right, steep canyon
on the left. Ahead I see the makeshift
settlement reminiscent
of the Sixties.

They've lashed some poles to make a bridge; a few
kids drop their fishing lines.

The tin-roofed houses glint
in Rinconada. A woman leaves her
pickup idling in the yard.
Cherries for sale.
The alcohol recovery center
sits on the edge of town,

not far from Gil's Garage.
Housetrailers line the road to Dixon and
El Quinto Sol, liquor
store and café.
In Embudo, the landmark's a stone house,
one window on the road.

Canyon walls and river
wind to a green plateau: farms and fruit stands.
The neat trees in the orchards
of Velarde
show how they run the water in at night
from the communal ditch.

Stark orange buttes and red
castles decorate land with uselessness
on the dry side of the road.
A cow. A horse.
Now animals graze on the scrubby plain
of San Juan Pueblo.

Kentucky Fried Chicken
begins the strip: Española, town of
fast food, unemployment lines.

The town mural
displays an Indian, an Hispanic and
an Anglo holding hands.

We've hiked the canyon walls
of Bandelier where the Stone Lions rest,
impassive gods. Snow spells cold
high in the bowl.
A sign for Los Alamos reminds me
of unspeakable things.

The home stretch: Santa Fe's
twelve miles, past Cuyamunge Saddlery
and Tesuque Pueblo.
What lies between
us is this landscape you have chosen: I
visit in the summer

like a fair-weather friend.
I reach the opera sign in the rain.
My wipers stick, but I climb
the final hill
past the new solar homes. I hear you scoff:
new houses everywhere.

My exit. The highway
rolls towards Albuquerque, another stretch.
Paseo de Peralta
takes me into town,
to you, so we may walk the plaza
and talk into the night.

THE NEW YEAR

This is the year you cannot reason with
or pull close like a lover.
This is the year you break off
like a chunk of bread, all of your charms
are useless here—black leather jacket,
dark glasses, fine boots—
and the saddle blanket you brought
to hang on the wall thinking
to retain the spirit of its maker.
This is the year of the body
restless, through nights of books
and self-recrimination. Not the body
of a young woman, but a woman
in the middle of her life, agitated,
shaking the chemicals in the beaker
to understand the mix, to find a use
for the precipitate.
This year the familiar vignettes
don't do the trick: horses pastured
on clear-cut fields, photographs of the high places
you climbed with friends, summer
houses against blue water.
Now you surrender
the pleasure of description, the known
subject, the religion of closure,
a soldier who puts down her weapons
and disarms in fear
straining to catch the rumors
of new borders and the undefended life.

YOM KIPPUR, TAOS, NEW MEXICO

I've expanded like the swollen door in summer
    to fit my own dimensions. Your loneliness

is a letter I read and put away, a daily reminder
    in the cry of the magpie that I am

still capable of inflicting pain
    at this distance.

Like a painting, our talk is dense with description,
    half-truths, landscapes, phrases layered

with a patina over time. When she came into my life
    I didn't hesitate.

Or is that only how it seems now, looking back?
    Or is that only how you accuse me, looking back?

Long ago, this desert was an inland sea. In the mountains
    you can still find shells.

It's these strange divagations I've come to love: midday sun
    on pink escarpments; dusk on gray sandstone;

toe-and-finger holes along the three hundred and fifty-seven foot
    climb to Acoma Pueblo, where the spirit

of the dead hovers about its earthly home
    four days, before the prayer sticks drive it away.

Today all good Jews collect their crimes like old clothes
    to be washed and given to the poor.

I remember how my father held his father around the shoulders
    as they walked to the old synagogue in Philadelphia.

"We're almost there, Pop," he said. "A few more blocks."
   I want to tell you that we, too, are almost there,

for someone has mapped this autumn field with meaning, and any day
   October, brooding in me, will open to reveal

our names—inscribed or absent—
   among the dry thistles and spent weeds.

KINDNESS

Now that my sister is dead I could say
I won, but as the eldest I didn't
show her kindness and now I have to live
out my life. I remember opportunities
for kindness, small things.
Because they never know when a god
might be disguised as an animal, people
in other countries—hurrying to corner shrines
to leave petals or light holy oil—
part with respect for the thin cattle.
They honor life in this form
because they know the sacred
takes many shapes but is nourished by kindness.

DEATH OF THE OWL

—for Pat Sargent

She said someone will come for the wings,
and snap them off, whole.
Someone for the claw, foot of a prayerstick.
Someone will come for the eyes,
like the woman from Cochiti Pueblo
who replaced her own with the raptor's.
Every part will be used:
the short tail feathers
that cover the arms and torso
of Owl Boy taken from his parents
and changed into a bird.
Nothing is wasted.
No time to stop, I said.
Right behind you, she replied, someone
who needed the feathers of the breast
to place beside the restless child
and induce sleep.
Someone who needed the undertail
feathers for a good peach crop.
I saw the wings lift,
heard the head crack,
no time to swerve—
the bird hunched in the highway
drawn by something dead in the road—
before she hurtled into the metal.
A shaman who required the feathers
for her hair was coming
to gain power over illness,
and someone claimed the remains
of the Burrowing Owl who lives in the underworld
and speaks with the dead.

Someone who wanted an audience
with the Bringer of Omens,
the Priestess of Prairie Dogs,
was coming, she said,
right behind you.

THE ROAST CHICKEN

When I set the roast chicken in the center
of the table and sat down, alone, to eat,
I understood the meaning of my life. That morning
when I squirted the lousy Cambridge water
into the coffee pot, I knew why my sister
took her life. The first night I ate
the roast chicken in honor of couples,
in honor of the labor and elegance of compromise.
The second night I ate the roast chicken weeping
with self-pity, because I had no partner to designate
on my health plan form, should I become incapacitated,
my life sustained solely by machines.
The third night I picked at the chicken
and considered how my life has been a flight
from family, and how I've arrived
at middle age without one.
Who will remember with me the old North Broad Street
train station? Who will bike with me to the drug store
in Mount Airy for my sister's medication? Who will know
the hatred I harbored for my father
who could not tolerate noise, and who will love me
now that I have become him, a person
who cannot tolerate noise? Who will ask me
about the Saturdays I wandered around Chestnut Hill
my senior year in high school
with a little money in my pocket,
looking at earrings and
developing expensive taste?
Now I watch my neighbors kneeling
in the early November cold to plant
their spring bulbs. Their faith amazes me,
for today I understand that by such deeds

human goodness is recognized.
All week the brick streets of Cambridge
have been saying *goodbye,* quietly, hushed
by leaves, like a lover who knows it's over
and speaks kindly, finally, in a café
before she disappears. And you're left
knowing that she was your best chance,
though she would say
your best chances are the ones you take.

NOTES

"Shopping": In the Southwest, the word "pawn" refers to jewelry or other collectables sold or pawned by the original makers or owners.

"The Crypto-Jews": During the fifteenth century, many Jews in Spain and Portugal disguised their identities by converting to Catholicism or by assuming Catholic religious practices. Generations later, their descendants, having grown up Catholic, discovered their buried histories.

"Peter Pan in North America": I am indebted to Marjorie Garber for her discussion of Peter Pan in *Vested Interests*.

"Contradancing in Nelson, N.H.": A contradance is a folk dance of English origin, performed in two lines with partners facing each other.

"The Ribbon": According to Jewish tradition, individuals in mourning wear a piece of black fabric rent by a rabbi.

Acknowledgments

The author and publisher thank the editors of the following publications in which these poems, several in earlier versions, previously appeared: *Agni Review* ("The Elimination of First Thoughts," "Haircut on Via di Mezzo"); *The American Poetry Review* ("A History of Sexual Preference," "In Pietrasanta," "Port-au-Prince, 1960," "The Roast Chicken," "Shopping"); *The Boston Review* ("Meeting the Gaze of the Great Horned Owl"); *Crab Orchard Review* ("Spiritual Morning," "The New Year"); *Global City Review* ("Bicycle Days," "My Grandmother's Crystal Ball"); *Harvard Magazine* ("Villanelle for a Lesbian Mom"); *The Harvard Review* ("We Thought of Each Other as Food"); *The Lesbian Review of Books* ("Peter Pan in North America"); *The Literary Review* ("The Crypto-Jews"); *New Virginia Review* ("Santo Domingo Feast Day"); *The Radcliffe Quarterly* ("The Mystery, Then the Facts");*Tampa Review* ("Family Romance," "Solar"); *13th Moon* ("From Taos to Santa Fe").

"Contradancing in Nelson, N.H." originally appeared in *The Kenyon Review*, vol. XIV, Winter 1992.

"The Star Show" originally appeared in *Ploughshares*, vol. 17/nos. 2 & 3.

Anthologies: *The Arc of Love: An Anthology of Lesbian Love Poems* ("Midnight Swim"); *The Four-Way Reader* ("The Crypto-Jews," "Death of the Owl," "Meeting the Gaze of the Great Horned Owl," "My Grandmother's Crystal Ball," "The Roast Chicken," "Shopping," and "We Thought of Each Other as Food"); *Saludos! Poems of New Mexico* ("Hold Back," "Shopping," and "Yom Kippur, Taos, New Mexico"). "Dreaming at the Rexall Drug" was first printed in the book *What Will Suffice: Contemporary American Poets on the Art of Poetry,* edited by Christopher Buckley and Christopher Merrill, published by Gibbs Smith, Publisher, 1995.

"The Ribbon" first appeared in *Her Face in the Mirror* by Faye Moskowitz, copyright © 1994 by Beacon Press, and is reprinted by permission of Beacon Press.

I thank the Ucross Foundation, the Virginia Center for the Creative Arts, and the Helene Wurlitzer Foundation of New Mexico for residencies during which I wrote some of these poems. A fellowship in poetry from the National Endowment for the Arts provided encouragement and precious time. For their steadfastness and love, I thank my parents. Thanks to Natalie Goldberg for sharing her house on the mesa and to Miriam Goodman for the cabin on the mowing. For assistance in shaping this manuscript, I thank Miriam Goodman, Susanna Kaysen, and Jane Miller. For research assistance, I thank Jane Knowles, the Radcliffe College archivist. I am grateful for the interest and support of my colleagues in the English Department at The Pennsylvania State University.

ROBIN BECKER ──────────────

is the author of *Personal Effects* (with Minton and Zuckerman), *Backtalk*, and *Giacometti's Dog*. She has received fellowships in poetry from the Massachusetts Artists Foundation, the National Endowment for the Arts, and the Bunting Institute of Radcliffe College (1995–1996). Her poems and book reviews have appeared in publications including *The American Poetry Review, Belles Lettres, The Boston Globe, The Boston Review, The Kenyon Review, Ploughshares, Prairie Schooner,* and *The Women's Review of Books*. She is a member of the Board of Directors of The Associated Writing Programs and serves as poetry editor for *The Women's Review of Books*. Robin Becker teaches in the MFA program at Pennsylvania State University where she is an Associate Professor of English.

Library of Congress Cataloging-in-Publication Data

Becker, Robin

All-american girl / Robin Becker
       p.   cm. —(Pitt Poetry Series)
     ISBN 0-8229-3917-7 (cl.).—ISBN 0-8229-5580-6 (pbk.)
     I. Title.   II. Series.
PS3552.E257C76   1996   95-21965
  811'.54—dc20   CIP